She/Her

poems by

Ellen Hernandez

Finishing Line Press
Georgetown, Kentucky

She/Her

Copyright © 2025 by Ellen Hernandez
ISBN 000-0-00000-000-0   First Edition
All rights reserved under International and Pan-American Copyright Conventions. No part of this book may be reproduced in any manner whatsoever without written permission from the publisher, except in the case of brief quotations embodied in critical articles and reviews.

ACKNOWLEDGMENTS

As a woman, I have encompassed so many roles: daughter, wife, mother, friend, teacher, writer, churchgoer, traveler, survivor, community-member, and so much more. This collection has been more than thirty years in the making, spanning many phases of my life. It would not have been possible without all the women in my life who have loved, supported, and encouraged me. The women with whom I taught for over 35-years, the women in my neighborhood, the PTA moms, my book club Pearls, my new and old friends near and far, the fellow writers, the women with whom I work at the High Atlas Foundation in Morocco, the women on my textbook editing team at Cognella Inc., the women in my family here and gone, all of whom have inspired me in ways small and big even when they were not aware. Foremost among all of them are my mother, Mary Ann Ewing Popolizio, whose courage willed me into being and whose unconditional love sustains me, and my daughter, Mia Bianca Hernandez, who saved my life and whose light and laughter illuminate the way for me. Thank you, ladies.

Publisher: Leah Huete de Maines
Editor: Christen Kincaid
Cover Art: Ellen Hernandez
Author Photo: Richard Hernandez
Cover Design: Elizabeth Maines McCleavy

Order online: www.finishinglinepress.com
also available on amazon.com

Author inquiries and mail orders:
Finishing Line Press
PO Box 1626
Georgetown, Kentucky 40324
USA

Contents

The Diver 1

Four O'clock January 3

Evening at the Philharmonic 4

Receipt from Grafton Street 5

Marriage Blueprint 7

This Was Harold's Favorite Hymn 8

Meditation on the Breath 9

Reminder 10

Recital 11

By the Light of the Moon 13

Signs of Life 14

Sandbox 16

The Poem I Do Not Have Time to Write 17

A Page for You 19

Losing Ben Torres 20

Writing 21

Moonstone 23

Her Feet 25

*To Donna
because it was your idea*

*Proceeds from this book will be donated to
breast cancer support and research*

Foreword

In the heart of the collection, *She/Her*, Ellen Hernandez weaves a tapestry of womanhood, capturing the essence of life's myriad roles and experiences. This anthology, a labor of love spanning over three decades, is a tribute to the women who have shaped, inspired and supported her journey.

For Donna [Armstrong], whose idea sparked this creation, and to all the women who have walked beside Ellen—mothers, daughters, friends, colleagues, and mentors—this book is a testament to their enduring influence. Each poem is a reflection of the shared moments, the silent struggles, and the triumphant joys that define the female experience.

From the tender recollections of childhood in "The Diver" to the poignant reflections on loss in "Losing Ben Torres," Ellen's words resonate with authenticity and grace. Her verses dance through the seasons of life, capturing the fleeting beauty of a January afternoon, the solemnity of a philharmonic evening, and the intimate whispers of moonlit nights.

This collection is more than poetry; it is a celebration of resilience and love. It is a journey through the landscapes of memory and emotion, where every line is a step towards understanding and every stanza a tribute to the strength of women. As you turn these pages, you may find echoes of your own story and the courage to embrace your unique path.

Welcome to *She/Her*—a poetic embrace of the feminine spirit, a heartfelt homage to the women who make us whole.

This collection is a must-read for anyone seeking to understand the multifaceted nature of being a woman.

Faleeha Hassan, December 2024, internationally-recognized, award-winning author of numerous poetry collections, including *A Goat in a Tequila Cup* (Finishing Line Press, 2024) and the memoir *War and Me* (Amazon Crossing, 2022).

The Diver

I glide, just skimming the surface,
eyes closed, nose plugged,
the water rolling over my boy-girl body
as I explode into July's twilight.

You, still in your work clothes
baked black from rolling out tar
will not suffer me to undertake this thing part way.
Bend your knees.

Again, I glide.
I hear the thumping of my chest amplified.
*Better—now try it from the back of the board,
and this time try to keep your feet together.*

Plop—Ooh, I know before I'm halfway to you
there was too much splash.
Slapping your splintered hands on your knees,
you shout, *It's a platform, not a springboard.
If you bounce, you'll crack it!*

My face must fall,
the way it does when you're nine
(and twenty-nine)
for you relent and offer,
Stay in the shallow end; we'll play a game,
retrieving loose change from your soiled pocket.

Down and down I dive until
I've earned at least a buck and a quarter.
When you hold out a towel,
I plead for more practice,
for your stubbornness is on me now,
like chlorinated beads.
C'mon, your lips are turning blue.

Even now, my teeth chattering,
clutching my arms to my sides
while I shiver before the world,
I wonder how you can help me, daddy,
to keep my feet steady, my body aligned,
my chin tucked under.

Four O'Clock January

Say that again.
>She shifts uneasily on the couch's prickly wool,
>pressing her cheek to the receiver.

Does that mean...?
>She covers the other ear to block out
>the overwhelming silence of the empty room,
>struggling to hear his voice.

But when did you...?
>The paint on the windowsill shows smudges and stains,
>and she turns away.

How long?
>The damp January draft trespasses through the pane
>to assault her face, already frozen.

Will you...?
>She swallows her breath now,
>holds it, prolongs it, refuses to release it,
>is paralyzed, numb, suffocating,
>but still she chokes it back,
>her hand to her brow.
>She hears the third chime.

Will you...?
>The clock collects itself and strikes.

Evening at the Philharmonic

Tonight, below pearly moon on blank canvas,
my breath comes fast and foggy
with February's crystals crunching underfoot.
In the concert hall, anticipation shakes off the chill,
replaced by warm overture.

House lights dimmed, the baton punctuates the air
and moody Sibelius stirs my still blood.
My fingers search the folds of coat and glove and skirt,
finally latching onto a cushioned arm.

Horns and strings embrace, blessed by Borodin.
A hum rises from the bows and weaves
through fingers, neck, and a flushed cheek,
through reed and tube, bending twice upon itself, entwined,
falling gently on instrument and player
to grateful intermezzo.
Respite is brief, permits bracing inhalation
for Ravel's furtive entrance
as, *poco a poco*, the Spanish dance intoxicates.

Pressing lips to embouchure pours sweet treacle,
caught by swelling clarinet,
and rising in vapor to caress the curve of violin.
Piccolo's shrill cry meets snare drum's cadence
and, in crescendo, all collapse.

Applause and *bravissimo!* startle me to presence,
The haunting echo of timpani still pulsing in my veins.

Receipt from Grafton Street

September, she found
an unexpected slip of paper,
a pocketed document,
proof of Spring in Dublin.
> *She walked on cobblestones,*
> *past vendors—*
> *flowers, bags, scarves, fruit.*
> *She watched an American play*
> *at Bewley's Pub—*
> *a woman, a man, a subway, death—*
> *and ate a thin, brown bread sandwich.*
> *She passed the shops and strolled the green,*
> *resting under a tree at Trinity,*
> *painted toenails with a small bottle from the chemist.*
> *The natives said she'd brought*
> *the only sun they'd have that season,*
> *their pink skin roasting*
> *as they dotted the landscape.*

Autumn, she rubbed the paper privately,
absorbing that other day
through her fingertips.

Marriage Blueprint

Make of your marriage a home such as this:
Found it on faith,
strong and evenly poured.
Frame it with support,
held square and true and plumb,
girdered in the right places
to carry the heaviest weight.

Let the joints be made tight,
yet allow for the flexibility
of the materials you use.
Insulate it with trust,
to provide warmth and protection
from the elements.

Fashion it with care,
that it will stand straight and right,
from the mortar to the plaster to the rafters.
Fill the maze of rooms
with tapestries of laughter, kindness, and compassion,
creating places of solitude and unity.
Build this home within your hearts,
that you may continually return to it
for comfort and sustenance.
Make of your love a surrounding garden,
blooming more lush and more fragrant each year.

Make of your marriage a home,
and build it to last forever.

This Was Harold's Favorite Hymn

The widows move
        on cue,
gold plates
        in withered hands.
Shrunken, sagging,
        cotton-haired,
they march
        unsteadily
        past pews,
heads bowed,
fingers entwined,
leaning willow trees.

They pad along the aisle,
        and whisper a memory.

Meditation on the Breath

Waking,
my shallow breath
unstrained
breaks into spasm,
a choking, liquid sputtering—
cement lungs
seize,
gasp,
cough, unable
to dislodge
stale air,
trapped—

a paralyzed hour of
this ...
relentless ...
dance.

Reminder

Notice this belly, the soft
Ornament between two promontory bones—
Bearing children should be easy.

Across the doughy flesh and downy fleece
Become acquainted with the inward arc,
Invitation to a toddler's perch.

Eclipse the scars of youth's diseases,
Salient flaws of a soil ready to be seeded,
Fertile land prone for harvest. Yet,

Obscured from hand or eye is the familiar
Reminder, the womb obliquely reversed,
Eluding the tangle of gauge and chart and
Limbs confounded, tugging, tugging at
Life twice come and gone. That putrid scent
Echoes a cruel taunt as it rises:
    No striated scars—
        No rounded pot—
            No tousled head beside.

Recital

Arms and feet in first position
        Back straight,
        cool countertop against
        my summer skin,
        I present cards
        and copays.

        Pink gown tied in front,
        feet dangling off the table,
        I fret over chipped
        nail polish, hum to
        piped-in Motown,
        await his entrance
        for a *pas de deux*.

Hand on the barre,
Feet apart in second,
Now grand plié
        Slide down to the end,
        discreet drape across hips:
        hard metal makes
        internal pirouettes,
        idle conversation
        an accompaniment.

Arms overhead in fifth
        Practiced fingers
        search flesh for signs
        of malady.

Relevé,
Jeté, jeté
        Change of costume
        and glide offstage:
        this,
        a compulsory, seasonal dance.

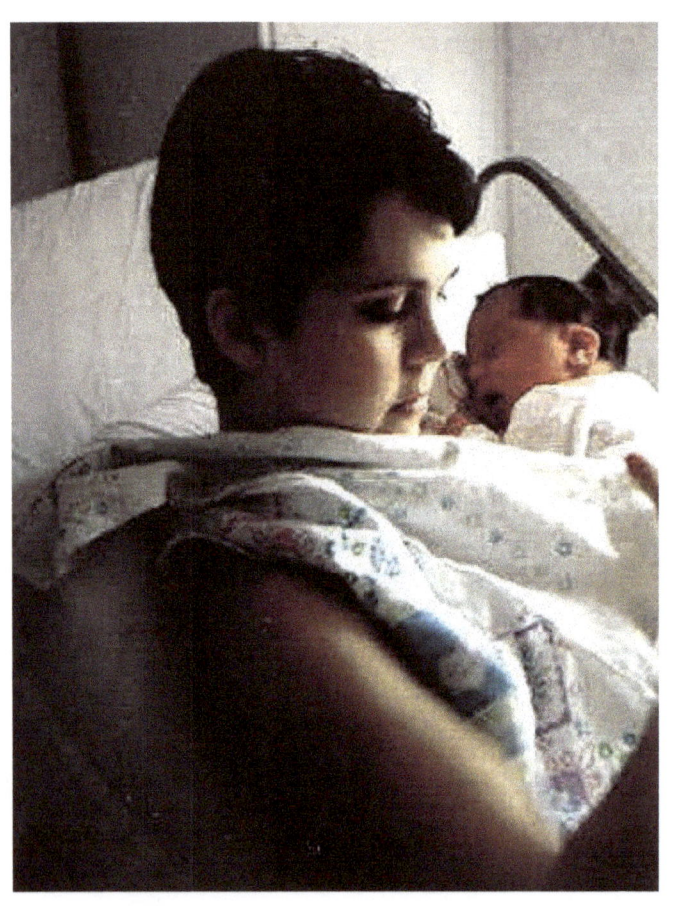

By the Light of the Moon

In the blue moonlight of two a.m.,
his hand incessantly
pried me open.
His breath was
wet in my ear.
He begged with urgency,
insisted with brutality.
His mouth pressed
hard against my face,
his heavy weight
crushing my chest.
I strained to move,
to breathe.
The walls were so cold
and so dark.

Another decade, another night,
the same uncanny blue moonlight,
my baby's fingers
like ribbons
curl around mine.
Her breath opens
my heart.
It soothes me,
like a whisper,
a lullaby.
Her mouth presses
softly against my skin.
Her feathery weight
tugs at my breast.
She gives me life,
awakens my soul.
The walls in this room are so new
and so warm.

How could the same moon shine then as now?

Signs of Life

Dried, salty trails
on the perfect hills and valleys
of your tiny, sleeping face
trace an earlier turmoil.

Headless, naked Barbies
testify to your tortured fury.

A pocketed pigtail holder,
a wrinkled candy wrapper,
a broken string of beads and used Band-Aid,
that insistent "Barney" tune
that lives in my head,
sandwich fragments in the fridge,
tattered drawings
and crayon stubs:

all a grafting of
your life
onto mine.

Sandbox

Perfect stillness
in sunlight,
the way the wind
lifts your hair
away from your angel face,
the way you scream
with delight
and cling
with desperate joy
to newfound friends:

I cry for
your full and fragile heart.

The Poem I Do Not Have Time to Write

12:30 a.m.—the end of my day.
Could not find a clean bra this morning,
so I went to work in a black lace bustier
and wondered if anyone could tell.
My daughter ate a fruit tart on the way to the sitter
and arrived with dirty hands and mouth.
(Holy Sh*t, I forgot to buckle her safety belt)
For me, it was drive-thru Burger King,
but at least I could wipe my own mouth.

Work is a five-hour blur where 1 in 10 students
have done their homework.
The pediatrician at 2:15… must leave at 1:45
(This is my mantra)
One more question.
One more late paper.
One more excuse.
I leave at 2:05.
On the way out of the parking lot, I recall the yogurt and apple
waiting for me in the faculty lounge fridge.
I hope my lunch bag is still there on Wednesday.
It's the extra trip to Dollar Tree I can't afford.

On my hands and knees outside the doctor's office
inspecting the damage to my car's belly
from the driveway bottom-out,
I remember the poem I've yet to write
for the workshop I need so badly.

Pulling her from the car seat
(Thank God, it's buckled)
I smell poop.
I'm saved. The sitter has packed an extra diaper in her bag
(though I have to use wet paper towels for wipes).
I'm late, but they take me,
demanding from across the full waiting room,
We need your copay.

She can't have her booster shot today because
she has an ear infection.
We'll have to come back in 10 days.
Stop at CVS with the prescription; have to pick it up later.

In the sanctuary of my home, I scream out—
once—
quickly—
just to relieve the pressure.
We read the mail,
pet the dog,
change our clothes,
play with blocks,
start the dinner,
not necessarily in that or any order.
By the time he comes home, I'm ready to pass the baton.

Seven hours later
in the stillness of a house asleep,
I sit in bed, pondering,
wanting to write of how my beloved child
saved me from a life of addiction,
or the losses and joys and passions I feel,
but I do not have the time.

A Page for You
    (after Theme for English B by Langston Hughes)

The student said,
*Why don't **you** go home and write
a page tonight?*

That's easy, right?
Thirty-four, Irish-Italian, born in Queens.
Moved to Long Island, then Boston, then here,
small-town New Jersey, across the highway,
down Haddon Avenue to Conard to Park,
up the front steps into a smaller house than
the one I grew up in,
too close to my neighbors,
but less anger and no one drunk.

If I am what I feel and see and hear, here in suburbia,
do I hear you in Camden?
I am small towns with white people,
without you, not wanting you, and not wanting my husband,
Puerto Rican, from Brooklyn.

Being me, this page will be white.
But it will be Puerto Rican from Brooklyn, too.
And it will be a part of you, student. You are not white—
yet a part of me, as I am a part of you.

Some days you don't want to be like me,
and you don't want to write in my English.
Some days perhaps you are tired, and want
to write in your own English, your own voice,
not mine, or not write at all, but speak,
because that is more a part of you.
Often, I do not want to be a part of you either,
but be the first me, who did not see and feel and
hear Camden.

I guess you learn from me, and I try to learn from you—
although you're younger—and not white—and less free.

Losing Ben Torres

His unreturned papers,
his name on my student roster,
stop me dead in my tracks.

From the podium,
I stare at his empty seat:
imagine large brown eyes,
close-cropped brown hair,
a gap-toothed smile,
the expression on his face
from the light of the open car door
just before
his head exploded onto the pavement.

Two Bens.
One in this room.
One lying on a Philly street.
Just another botched robbery
on the evening news,
but he wrote A papers.
Later, in the parking lot,
I glance over my shoulder,
unlock the car,
remove the steering Club.
As deliberately as any other day,
I push down the lock.

Does it matter that
Ben was the robber?
Maybe.
But do you see as I do
the flash of metal
as it cuts down
a mother's hopes and dreams?
As it slices through
the poet, the husband, the father
      he might have been?

Writing

You tell me to rest,
not to stay up
writing.
I tell you I won't
and mean what I say
at the time.
But now that I've said it,
I feel compelled
to write
about writing.

You think
I write a lot,
but I don't
write enough.
Time must be devoted
every day.
It can't be helped
or controlled
or put to rest.

I am always
composing
in my head, so
when you see me
with pen and paper
that's only half
the writing
I'm doing.

I will stop when I run out of
ink
or when my hand is too
cramped
to go on.

Moonstone

We cruised along the coast on a sunny Monday
    beside the laughing ocean—
        delighted waves dashing black rocks on
    Moonstone Beach.
Elephant seals sent showers of sand with fingerlike flippers,
    a Piedras Blancas repose
        broken by bulls in a dominance dance.

Wind lightly kissed our cheeks
    as we sat seaside,
        Hearst's Paso Robles chardonnays
    sticky sweet in stemware.
Where Californians promenaded at shore's edge,
    dogs and children skipped in waves:
        their wonderment an artist's prize.

We hugged the highway's curves,
    drawn north by diamonds beaming on blue.
Big Sur's mountain majesty cascaded like a waterfall,
    near amber hills and turquoise waters,
        a twisting path to Paradise.
We climbed the cliff to Nepenthé,
    opium for a yearlong suffering.
Saint Lucia's peaks gave warm embrace,
    a panorama of pines and palms,
    breeze and birdsong,
    waves and wonder.
The Camino Real's music met our fish-and-fillet feast—
    a serenade to *vida, corazón, y alma*
        'midst light and shadows of a Golden Hour.

All who pass and all who stay,
    who came before and who come after—
    tú y yo—are lured
    by smell of salt, of sage,
    of the sound of the sea.

'round a bend, the celestial stone appeared,
    her face parting night's dark curtain.
Luna y Madre Tierra lleva me hacia el mar,
    una niña siempre seré.
The full moon lit our way
    and led us home.

Her Feet

She has her mother's feet,
      long and wide,
      poised for flight.
Long-ago yesterday,
      pressed urgently
      beneath a rib they
      made her presence known.
Those early days,
      delicious digits beckoned
      to be swallowed whole.
Years since, they
      danced in mother's dress-up,
      stamped in fits of fury,
      scurried through summer grass,
      hurried down school halls,
      peeked under fitting rooms,
      squeaked up late night stairs.
Today, facing firmly forward,
      her own feet, poised to run,
      poised for flight,
      take off toward tomorrow.

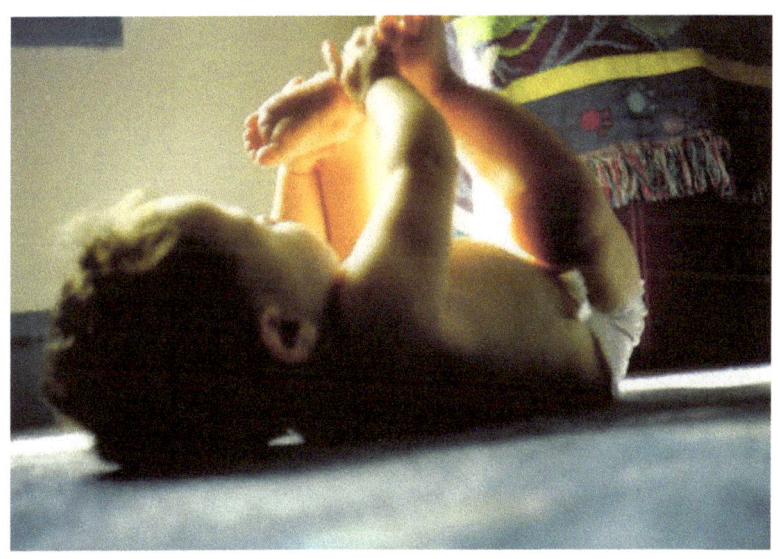

Ellen Hernandez is a freelance writer and retired English professor who lives in southern New Jersey. Her chapbooks of poetry include *In Morocco* and *Voices from a Pandemic* (Finishing Line Press). Among her other publications are a college composition textbook, *Writing for All* (Cognella, Inc.) and recent articles in *Peace Review Journal of Social Justice, Environmental Challenges,* and *Media for Freedom.* She also devotes part of her time to projects of sustainable human development with the High Atlas Foundation, a U.S.-Moroccan non-profit organization, and to speaking engagements in the New York-New Jersey-Pennsylvania region

www.ingramcontent.com/pod-product-compliance
Lightning Source LLC
Chambersburg PA
CBHW040308170426
43194CB00022B/2942